Beauty in Br

A Hopeful Handbook for the Early Years as a Special Needs Parent

by Kathy McClelland

Beauty in Broken Dreams
A Hopeful Handbook for the Early Years as a Special Needs Parent

Copyright © 2017 by Kathy McClelland

Cover Design: Kathy McClelland
Editors: Diane Krause, Ellen Tuthill
Author Photo Credit: Marti Smith
Photography: March of Dimes and Markum Photography

Disclaimer: The information provided in this book isn't guaranteed to be accurate. It is based on the author's knowledge, experience, and opinion.

www.kathymcclelland.com

Scripture quotations marked NASB are taken from the New American Standard Bible Copyright © 1960, 1962, 1963, 1968, 1971, 1972, 1973, 1975, 1977, 1995 by The Lockman Foundation. Used by permission. (www.Lockman.org)

Scripture quotations marked NET are taken from the New English Translation. NET Bible® Copyright ©1996-2006 by Biblical Studies Press, L.L.C. http://netbible.com All rights reserved.

Scripture quotations marked NIV are taken from

To Nathan, my unexpected blessing.

I am grateful for the many ways you've enabled me to see
true beauty and lasting hope.

INTRODUCTION

The moment Nathan was born I knew something was wrong. His cry was a dead giveaway. Within two weeks we had a diagnosis. The cut was deep and clean. I never allowed myself to know him as the child I had hoped and dreamed he would be when he was still in utero. Ever since the day I met him, he has been my son with special needs.

For parents who slowly uncover their child's disabilities, I imagine it's like a chronic wound. It won't heal. As soon as it starts to scab over it's broken open all over again. The scar tissue keeps growing thicker and thicker.

Everyone's story is different. Although this story is written from the perspective of uncovering my child's special needs diagnosis at birth, I hope it contains practical and encouraging insights for whatever your story, wherever you're at, and wherever you're going.

You may be wondering, is it over yet? The first year is especially painful, grueling, and you question if you will ever be the same again. For many, a special needs diagnosis marks a line in the sand. It marks who you were before your child's diagnosis and who you are after.

I know I am not the same person. I made my way through the first year of Nathan's life stumbling around in the dark, trying to assess the wreckage of our family, bumping into roadblocks and hitting dead ends. I began to see glimmers of light and hope along the way. God was taking something I deemed as awful and making something beautiful. I can see it more clearly now. He was not changing my circumstances. He was redirecting and transforming me.

He was making something beautiful out of my broken dreams.

OUR STORY

For You formed my inward parts;

You wove me in my mother's womb.

I will give thanks to You, for I am fearfully and wonderfully made;

Wonderful are Your works,

And my soul knows it very well.

My frame was not hidden from You,

When I was made in secret,

And skillfully wrought in the depths of the earth;

Your eyes have seen my unformed substance;

And in Your book were all written

The days that were ordained for me,

When as yet there was not one of them.

How precious also are Your thoughts to me, O God!

How vast is the sum of them!

- Psalm 139: 13-17 (NASB)

An Unusual Pregnancy

We had no plans to conceive. In fact, we were in the middle of the adoption process. We wanted a second baby, but baby number one had presented a difficult and dangerous pregnancy.

When I took a pregnancy test for my second child, I was beyond shocked. My husband was out of town. It took me several hours before I called to tell him the news.

Silence on the other end of the phone.

Sure, we were excited. We were cautiously optimistic. I had had two pulmonary emboli with my first baby, Mac, due to clotting disorders. Then Mac arrived six weeks early after an abruption from pre-eclampsia and HELLP syndrome.

We were hesitant to get too happy for baby number two. Maybe justifiably so. When I went to the OB for my confirmation of pregnancy appointment, my HCG levels weren't what they should be. After two more blood draws, I was informed that my levels still weren't rising and I would likely miscarry before twelve weeks.

That was a scary and confusing time. How could we be given this baby we wanted, but weren't expecting, and now just wait for him to pass on?

Well I didn't miscarry. Around ten weeks I went in for a repeat ultrasound. As soon as it registered I immediately noticed the egg sac looked bigger than the week before. And there on the screen right before my very eyes was a beating heart.

That very same morning, a verse from a daily devotional appeared on my husband's phone: "But God chose the foolish things of the world to shame the wise; God chose the weak things of the world to shame the strong" (1 Corinthians 1:27 NASB). Just as that verse said, God was shaming the human medical knowledge which said this baby wasn't going to survive.

Next I just waited for the nausea, heartburn and general uncomfortable feeling to settle in. And it did.

But all along something was different about this baby. I didn't know, yet I knew. Everyone in my family kept saying, "God has a plan for this baby." And boy did He ever.

At twenty weeks I went in for a sonogram. The tech became quiet and said she needed to have the doctor come in and look at the screen. Nathan had a two-vessel cord. The tech said that it can sometimes be linked to chromosomal abnormalities and low birth weight babies. She tried to assure us that most of the doctor's two-cord babies were average to large sized. When the doctor arrived and viewed the sonogram he told us Nathan was growing like a weed, I let that set my mind at ease. I took him at his word that everything would be fine.

We declined further testing, and in the end, I'm grateful we did. It was the right decision for us. I can't imagine knowing of Nathan's birth defects before he was born. It would have put my body through much unnecessary stress. The only way out of the pregnancy was to terminate. That wasn't an option we would have chosen for our family based on our belief that every life has value. Even though I wouldn't have chosen my pregnancy, now I completely understand the emotions of women who so desperately want a way out.

Not knowing Nathan's diagnosis in utero allowed me to enjoy my pregnancy, as much as you can enjoy a pregnancy, without knowing that I had a little baby growing inside me who would change the trajectory of our lives forever.

When You Suspect Something is Wrong

There were indicators that something might be wrong with Nathan, but my body was handling the pregnancy better than expected. Later my sister would remind me of a phone call when I confessed to her, "I think I'm going to be fine, but I worry that something may be wrong with the baby." Toward the end of my pregnancy red flags were popping up like crazy. I was admitted twice for having frequent contractions and decreased fetal movement. They checked out at the hospital as false starts and I was sent home.

I went to the perinatologist for the stress test, and Nathan failed them twice. We would sit and wait in the doctor's office for hours, just willing this little baby to practice his breathing. Those ultrasound techs must have years of practice in trying to calm anxious mothers. They repeatedly said things like, "These babies don't like to do what we want them to do. We just need to wait." And wait we did. We waited for something to go wrong with me like it did with my first delivery. It never did. This time it was my baby's medical drama that was about to unfold before us.

At thirty-seven weeks, my OB said, "Looks like you're having a baby." So I immediately headed over to the hospital. I waited one day under observation. The countdown to delivery was packed full of sweet moments. Even though I was hooked up to monitors and stationed in bed, I was thrilled. My husband was there trying to finish up some details with work, but distracted with anticipation. My parents had come to help. It was finally time.

My mom and dad brought my three-year-old, Mac, to my hospital room. We got to wait together. These were the final few hours we had as a happy family waiting for the next member to introduce himself to us. I was so proud. Proud of my husband for being such a good daddy. I was excited to watch him do it all over again. I was proud of the good big brother my son was going to become. And I was just excited that my parents were there this time—they missed Mac's birth because he came barrelling into the world too early. This time they were both here and it was perfect. I couldn't wait to make them grandparents again.

As I walked myself down the hall into the OR I was scared, anxious, excited, and eager to get it all over with. Pregnancy is not my forte and I was expecting this delivery would be a grand celebration of the end of that season of my life.

Strapped down on the table for my C-section, various people working in the room were upbeat and chatty. We were talking about my previous delivery of Mac and everything that went wrong. I told them that this baby was not in the plan. He was a surprise. We were in the process of adopting when I became pregnant. I'll never forget that one of the technicians said, "Well honey, you can make all the plans you like but there's Somebody else upstairs who's pulling all the strings." That statement would later become so significant to me. In fact, I clung to it in some of my darkest hours. I needed to believe that though this wasn't my plan, it was Somebody's. And He had this whole thing under control in a way that I didn't.

I delivered a five-pound, nine-ounce baby boy. We called him Nathan, which means "God has given."

My baby's first cry was weak and strange. He had an unusual spot on the back of his head, which I dismissed as a birth mark. We awaited APGAR scores. Though it seemed to take forever, they came back fine.

Generally Nathan appeared to have a very mellow attitude. He was not at all interested in nursing. He struggled to get the amniotic fluid out of his lungs. He was very spitty and bubbly and seemed to have a hard time managing all of the extra secretions in his mouth.

That night I looked over to his crib and realized he had turned blue. My husband simultaneously suctioned his throat and pulled the call button. Our son was choking and couldn't keep his temperature up so off he went to the NICU.

We began to suspect something more was wrong, but tried to talk ourselves out of it. His ears weren't really *that* low set. The slant of his eyes wasn't *that* noticeable. In fact, he seemed to resemble my husband's baby pictures.

I made excuses for things. He could just be small.

I blamed myself. Maybe we were too anxious for him to arrive and took him out too soon.

Eventually I would begin to bargain, "God, if you will heal my baby then I will tell everyone about You and the miracle You did."

Two weeks later, when the geneticist sat us down and said, "We did find something," I exhaled deeply. It was confirmed. There was no going back now. She went on to tell us that he would be severely intellectually disabled. She said that I would need help to care for him because I might not even be able to leave his side long enough to get a shower. In her words, "Maybe he'll walk. Maybe he'll talk. You will be living with an adult child unless you decide to put him in a group home." We got a lot of information in that meeting, yet walked away with less hope than I've ever felt before. So many medical words were thrown around which meant nothing to me. Even my husband, who has a medical background as a pediatric physician assistant, asked many questions and had a hard time piecing it all together. It was very disorienting.

Dealing with a New Diagnosis

The first few days post-diagnosis, time slowed down. I remember having dinner outside at a restaurant near the hospital with my husband days after Nathan was diagnosed. We barely ate anything. I sat with a blank stare on my face as I watched several "normal" kids running around kicking a soccer ball with their father. All of the dreams I had for my child had just been taken from me. We would never be that family. We would be lucky if Nathan would ever walk, let alone run after a ball. Life as I knew it came to a screeching halt. Everything that I had expected, hoped, depended on before, was gone. I had to adapt accordingly. But I didn't know how. Even worse: I didn't know if I wanted to.

This was the dark side. The time of intense grief. Grief so powerful it's visceral. I felt it in my heart, my stomach, my bones and sinew, all the way down to a cellular level in my body. I look back on it and don't know how I continued pumping breast milk. My physical body just wanted to shut down completely. But I had to keep going for the sake of both of my sons. For the one I had at home and for the one I didn't know if I would ever take home from the hospital.

Nathan's birth marked a before and after in my life. Before Nathan I was an at-home mom with one little boy and ready for a new baby. After Nathan I was grief stricken, heavy burdened, and constantly wondering what would become of our family. His birth was supposed to be a happy occasion, a reason for celebration. But it was the opposite. It sent me spiraling into an abyss of grief. Our world was turned upside down and we started bearing the burden of a life of disability long before he left the hospital.

I didn't know it at that time, but life would go on. It would become beautiful. The that season of brokenness would yield blessings found only in only in the work of God.

Blessed are the poor in spirit, for theirs is the kingdom of heaven. Blessed are those who mourn, for they shall be comforted. - Matthew 5:3-4 (NASB)

LIFE IN THE NICU

As he went along, he saw a man blind from birth. His disciples asked him, "Rabbi, who sinned, this man or his parents, that he was born blind?"

"Neither this man nor his parents sinned," said Jesus, "but this happened so that the works of God might be displayed in him.

- John 9:1-3 (NIV)

Life in the NICU

No mother hopes her baby ends up in the neonatal intensive care unit, but after spending a couple of hours with Nathan I was actually relieved when they sent him upstairs to the NICU. He wasn't doing normal baby things, like breathing, eating, and keeping his temperature. I knew the experts would be better able to care for him up there.

The NICU is intense. I felt it, not just the first time, but every time I visited my babies. Between my two kids, I've been a visiting parent at three different NICUs. Mac was six weeks premature and stayed in the NICU three weeks. Nathan, although technically full-term, was sick from the get-go and started in the NICU of his delivery hospital until he was a month old. He was then transferred to the local children's hospital where he could be under the care of sub-specialists for another month.

Each visit felt a little bit like this:

> *I slowly approach a wired glass window still tender from my incision. I give the receptionist my secret security code—a number that identifies me as my child's mother—and I wait for her to buzz me in. I'm eager to be with my baby, but equally nervous to know how I'll find him. As soon as the double doors unlock and swing wide open, I step across the threshold and into a different world. A world of tiny, fragile babies, fighting to overcome their initial battles in this life.*

> *It is often quiet, with the exception of intrusive monitors beeping intermittently and the constant flow of oxygen. Surprisingly, there is not much crying and if there is, it's not loud. These babies are too tiny, too sick.*

> *I am grilled by the front staff to ensure that I am not ill and haven't been around anyone who is. The gatekeepers do their best to keep anyone, even the mothers, from bringing in viruses from the*

outside.

There are rules to follow. The first and most sacred is scrubbing in at the sink. It's not like hand washing at the kitchen sink, it's like hand washing for surgery. There is a timer glaring at me to ensure that I scrub under my fingernails for the full three minutes. Three minutes is a long time to wash when all I want is to hold my bundle.

At the sink my tired, worn eyes meet with another momma. We are connected because both of our babies are on that same hidden floor of the hospital. We compare things like lugging around breast milk, but we know enough not to ask many specific questions for fear of different outcomes. Maybe one will be good and one bad.

I get to my son's bedside. A quick update from his nurse leaves me to piece together the rest of the hours he's been there, without me by his side. At least I know how much he ate, when and if he pooped, and how much weight he gained. I get updates on whether he stopped breathing or if his heart rate or oxygen levels dropped too low. All these important things and I missed them. I try to ease my guilt and believe he was sleeping most of the time anyway because that's what newborn babies do.

I lean in closely and begin whispering motherly things about how sweet and precious he is and how I'll love him forever. Then I begin the process of slowly collecting wires and carefully lifting him out of his warmer bed. His nurse helps me get comfortably settled into a reclining chair and tucks us up together with a bunch of freshly warmed hospital blankets. I'm doing the only thing I can for him. Holding him. We cuddle there for hours.

It doesn't take long to learn the daily routine of the NICU. Everything happens on a schedule: the feeding, the bathing, the therapist appointments, and the doctor's rounds. There is a system for everything: changing a diaper, marking breast milk, and adjusting monitor leads. I learned to take on the role of a nurse in many ways. I learned where the leads went and how to fix them if they weren't working properly. I juggled how to lift my baby out of his bed along with the multiple wires tethered to him. How to weigh a wet diaper. How to give a bath in one of those little pink hospital tubs. Where to find fresh baby blankets and new pacifiers. As much as it could, the NICU began to feel like a second home.

At the children's hospital Nathan's room was just around the corner from the sink where visitors were to scrub in. I would peek around to see what was going on as I scrubbed my hands. Sometimes, I could hear his distinctive cry. It was an awful, painful cry. It broke my heart. Often there was a nurse comforting him. I only remember arriving once when no one was holding him during a crying spell. If I didn't hear him upon my entry, I would check the monitors over the sink. Even as a non-medical person I became very good at reading his monitors to determine whether he was awake or asleep, based on his heart rate, even before I set foot in his room.

In the NICU you are encouraged to leave your baby under the constant care and vigilance of the nurses and go take care of yourself. It's a tricky balance as a mother. Instinctively you want to be close to your newborn but it's emotionally and physically exhausting to be there all the time. Finding that balance is something that you learn navigate throughout the time your baby is in the NICU.

At the beginning when you are in the hospital as a patient yourself, it's easy to spend all your time there. Once you are discharged it quickly gets complicated, especially if you have other children at home.

When Nathan was born I found myself needing to hold him as much as possible. We were being bombarded with information about his diagnosis and disabilities. It was too much for me to bear all at once. My mind couldn't comprehend the fact that this tiny, innocent, sweet little baby contained all of these broken, complicated issues - his heart was malpositioned, he had high-grade kidney reflux, he had a strange spot on the back of his head that looked like his brain was growing out on the MRI, he had a hard time stretching out his arms and legs, and the hardest part for me as mom: he couldn't nurse or take a bottle without aspirating. When I thought about the future—if he survived his medical complications—I couldn't help but think of how I would have a dependent adult child on my hands. In order for me to enjoy the moment of his baby sweetness and bond to him, I needed to just be sitting by his bedside holding him as much as possible.

My firstborn needed me as well. When he was with me, he wanted all of me and no one else. He came down to the hospital for visits almost daily. We would explore the hospital courtyards together, the cafeteria, and even my hospital room was a place of play for him. He would turn the hospital bed into a firetruck and we would pretend together. He pretending to be a fireman, me pretending that I was once again just his mom.

Since Nathan was in the NICU for two months, we found a rhythm where I would go in to visit Nathan early in the morning before Mac woke up. This avoided another painful goodbye for Mac. I would simply sit and hold Nathan all morning and on into the afternoon. My parents would bring Mac down to the hospital for lunch so that we could be together on campus for a while. We would have dinner together as a family. Then we would go home and do the normal bedtime routine together. Then do it all over again the next day.

Practical Tips for the NICU

Being organized in the midst of living in two places at the same time is essential. Part of you is back at home with the rest of your family. But that tiny little baby that was tucked inside you not that long ago, is still living in the hospital.

When Nathan was in the NICU, there were so many things that I was toting back and forth from the hospital daily. The essential items included:

- Paperwork (insurance papers, specialist information, business cards, etc.)
- Camera/phone
- Snacks and water bottle
- Baby clothes and blankets (which also meant laundry bags so I could bring things home and wash them)
- Breast pump and bottles
- Medium sized cooler to carry breast milk back and forth
- Journal, my most prized possession during those NICU days

My journal was extremely important during this time because I saw it as both my therapist and my memory. In the front of it I was constantly scribbling down my thoughts, feelings and corresponding Scriptures to comfort me. In the back of it I wrote down notes on possible diagnoses and specialists and other resources—things that I couldn't hold in my head but needed to remember. That journal was a great tool for me in the early days of emotional chaos and intense grief.

Finally, you may want to find a great big tote bag and a system for keeping track of everything. It will keep you slightly more sane especially when you feel like a crazy momma hopped up on hormones. I especially like the Thirty-One totes. Thirty-One has a file folder insert which I kept important paperwork in and I could easily insert in and out of different tote bags depending on what I needed to transport for the day.

He alone is my rock and my salvation; He is my fortress; I will never be shaken. - Psalm 62:2 (NIV)

I wrote this verse on an index card and one of the NICU nurses offered to tape it to the wall by Nathan's crib. I still have this card. It is now tucked between the pages of my Bible with the medical tape she used to tape it to the wall, folded over the edge. A memorial, a stone of remembrance to our time in the NICU.

Unexpected Emotions in the NICU

When Nathan was transferred to the children's hospital he had his own private NICU room. Under ordinary circumstances I would have preferred to stay in an open bay setting so that I could connect with other moms, but once we knew the severity of his diagnosis, having our own room was especially helpful. However even with the private rooms, the nurses had to keep other patients' monitors in our baby's room. If another baby was having a bad day, you felt it.

I'll never forget one afternoon. The baby in the room next door started dipping rapidly. Our eyes glued to the monitor as we watched her oxygen level drop. We watched it go from the high eighties all the way down to eleven percent. My eyes met my husband's. We knew what it meant. Next thing, nurses and respiratory therapists were running down the hall and the monitors began beeping more loudly than usual. They worked on her, on and off, that whole day long. They ended up putting in a breathing tube and the next day she went to the OR for a tracheostomy.

That baby was trying to die that day. We had seen Nathan's oxygen levels crash like hers, though not as quickly and persistently. I knew that other kids with Nathan's syndrome had trachs. I was suddenly overcome by the terror that that could have been my son. Even though we didn't see all that happened to the neighboring patient, we felt it deeply. It hit very close to the heart of our situation.

Having a NICU baby completely changed my perspective on life, particularly the beginning of life. When a baby is born they are supposed to be perfect and unblemished, no defects, completely untainted by the world. When you have a baby who immediately demonstrates that he is too weak or too sick, you realize how much in this world is broken. Some little souls are forced to be courageous before they're even equipped. That was what was most unexpected to me. Most heartbreaking. Things like breathing and eating are so basic to human life. My son was struggling with both of them and it turned my world upside down.

Surrounded by the brokenness in the bodies of these babies, my heart began to open to the hope of heaven in a whole new way. A place of perfection—of no more pain, tears, and sickness—that I longed for more than ever before.

Therefore we do not lose heart. Though outwardly we are wasting away, yet inwardly we are being renewed day by day. For our light and momentary troubles are achieving for us an eternal glory that far outweighs them all. So we fix our eyes not on what is seen, but on what is unseen, since what is seen is temporary, but what is unseen is eternal. - 2 Corinthians 4:16-18 (NIV)

Support in the NICU

The nurses were my biggest support while Nathan was in the hospital. My husband joked that in addition to being RNs, nurses really needed a counseling degree. Nurses we never knew before turned into some of our closest confidants. They listened to our fears, witnessed our tears, and handed us lots of tissues. So did some of the doctors. Never before have I trusted people that I knew nothing about with such raw and unfiltered emotion. In some ways it was a relief that I could process so much with them without feeling like I was burdening a friend or a family member.

While Nathan was inpatient I also began to look for support through outside organizations. March of Dimes was very involved in our hospital system. Their staff provided a special source of support. They organized and coordinated get-togethers for families. They helped us with simple projects—things that I would not have been able to do while we were in the NICU. One was a premade baby scrapbook. All I had to do was insert the pictures and hospital memorabilia. March of Dimes also arranged for a photographer to come into the NICU and take pictures of our family together. This was especially important to me. I wanted to have a professional capture some of my baby's newest days, even if he was still in the hospital.

Photo courtesy of March of Dimes

Once we left the hospital, I needed more ongoing support from the trauma of being in the NICU. I reached out to an organization called <u>Hand to Hold</u>, a local non-profit. One of the programs I was especially interested in was their peer-mentoring program. They matched me with a mom who had actually been in the very same NICUs with her son almost ten years prior. She came to visit me and listened to all of my emotions and fears. She told me things that no one else could say without having walked the path before me.

In the NICU you are somewhat sheltered from your new reality since others are sharing the burden of caring for your child. I didn't know if I had what it would take to be not just Nathan's mom, but his caregiver once I was doing this at home. I still had lots to learn. The time finally came when I was kicked out of the NICU nest.

The Lord will fight for you; you need only to be still. - Exodus 14:14 (NIV)

(Note: A list of local and national resources that may be available to you can be found in the <u>Appendix</u>.)

LIFE AT HOME

But he said to me, "My grace is sufficient for you, for my power is made perfect in weakness." Therefore I will boast all the more gladly about my weaknesses, so that Christ's power may rest on me. That is why, for Christ's sake, I delight in weaknesses, in insults, in hardships, in persecutions, in difficulties. For when I am weak, then I am strong.

- 2 Corinthians 12:9-11 (NIV)

Transitioning to Life at Home

As we got ready to leave the NICU, I was faced with the question, "What is our new normal?" I felt challenged to create a balance between my old life and my new life. I feared how this would play out practically. I feared the inevitable changes in my relationships, my independence, my needs, my schedule and day-to-day activities. I thought that I was going to hate my new life.

Everyone would say to me, "The first year is the hardest." I'm not quite ready to say that's true because I don't know what's ahead for our child and our family. I do know that it was hard. Very hard. What's different is that although the grief does sucker-punch me at times, it's no longer the constant overwhelming tidal wave of emotions that leaves me struggling to come up for air. Initially it was very visceral. I felt crushed by the weight of the pain and grief caused by having a child with disabilities. Now a wave of sadness rushes over me I can sit with it for a moment, feeling the weight of it but then move on, remembering the good my son's disability has also brought to my life.

As we transitioned to life at home—which I called the "the planted pot" phase—I tried desperately to enjoy all the baby moments as I attempted to settle back into my own cozy environment. His delays and medical complications weren't fully apparent yet, so while he was disabled, much of our experience was very normal—his smell, the sweet cuddles, his long afternoon naps, bundling him up in baby blankets for a fall walk, letting him sleep in my arms while we were out to dinner, and the midnight wake-up calls. The things that were different about him, primarily the feeding tube, were things that we were adjusting to. It was hard but I wanted to experience all of them.

So on the days that we didn't have therapy or doctor's appointments or insurance phone calls to make, I cuddled up on the couch with my little bundle while I watched my firstborn play Legos and make up stories about firemen rescuing people from burning buildings. It was amazing. And every bit the same as if I didn't have a baby with special needs. It wasn't that I was ignoring or in denial of who my son was. It was just that I wanted to soak up each and every moment of his babyhood because I knew his life would become very different. It was the slow ease into special needs for me as his mother. I had one foot in my old life and one foot in my new life.

Personal Inventory of Priorities

I quickly realized that life would not return to how it was before Nathan was born. Rather than resist the changes, I took an inventory of what I could **keep doing** and what I needed to **let go of**—at least in the short-term—and also what I desperately needed to **fight to maintain** in my life.

- Keep Doing but Do Different: Cooking healthy meant making easy fresh meals but not all the time. I began freezing meals and stopped being ashamed to serve the same thing twice for dinner in one week. I also began to better divide and conquer essential administrative tasks with my husband (things like paying bills, making phone calls to doctors and insurance companies).

- Let Go Of: Yard work, cleaning my house, various mom group gatherings, book club, and working out (short-term only, long-term working out is definitely a fight-to-hold-onto for me).

- Fight to Hold Onto: Writing, reading my Bible, and getting away by myself for coffee even if for a little bit.

It was very helpful for me to jot these things down. That way, when I got overwhelmed about everything I had to manage, I had already decided in advance what I would still do, what I outsourced, and what I stopped doing altogether.

I encourage you to start a list of your priorities by taking inventory of the responsibilities on your plate:

❑ Keep Doing, but Do Different:

❑ Let Go Of:

❑ Fight to Hold Onto:

Discovering Your New Normal One Day at a Time

Accepting your "new normal" doesn't happen quickly, at least it didn't for me. Once I realized that I didn't need to accept everything about my son's disabilities immediately, I felt more free. I didn't want my fear of the future to rob me of sweet moments with my baby. After all, you can't get that first year back. So I tried to adopt a "one day at a time" mentality. Enjoying today. Doing what I needed to do to make it through today and trusting God for what I needed in the future.

This has been something I've had to preach to myself over and over again. I tend to live in the future. I'm constantly trying to plan and prepare for what's to come. For me to live in the moment and deal with the present is much harder. And honestly, I didn't think there was much good that could come from a baby with special needs, especially as he got older and I envisioned all of the extra effort and resources he would require. I realized if I didn't stay in the moment, then life was going to pass right by before I could even enjoy what I was preparing for.

During that first year of Nathan's life I reconnected with a friend of mine who had a child with Down syndrome. I wanted to tap into all of her knowledge and experience and emotions that come with having a child with special needs. Shortly after we reconnected, she got a devastating diagnosis. Breast cancer. The worst kind. Her diagnosis hit me especially hard. Not just because she was my friend whom I loved, but also because it enforced a truth I already knew, but didn't want to believe. That is, there is no cap on the amount of hard things that you may have to endure during your lifetime. You don't reach a quota and then you stop dealing with hard things.

The Fear of the Future is Often Worse Than the Experience Itself

Once again it put me in that place of fearing the future and not engaging the moment. However, in the midst of her illness she said some things I will remember forever. One is that "the fear of the future is often worse than the experience itself." This is true because we can build something up to be such a monster in our heads. It's awful and terrible and scary. And God is not there in that imaginative nightmare we've created. Psalm 42 says that God is an ever *present* help in trouble. He's in the moment you're living presently. He's gone before you too but you are not omnipresent like God. You are able to only live in one place at a time. And that's right now.

There is an Upside to Every Circumstance

The second thing she told me that has stuck is "there is an upside to every circumstance." After her chemotherapy, she said, "I'd rather have hair, but there are upsides to not having hair." And I've translated that to "I'd rather have my child eat by mouth, but there are upsides to a g-tube." He can eat in the car. I can feed him overnight. I can easily hand him over to someone else to hold since I'm not nursing him. I don't have to cook elaborate baby foods or cut up food into super small pieces. There are upsides.

Things that aren't normal eventually become normal to you because you do them over and over again. You master them and incorporate them into your life and routine. And it works for your family. If you can get past the stares and the judgments of other people, then you can embrace the beauty of different and see God's blessings in your new normal.

> *You make known to me the path of life: you will fill me with joy in your presence, with eternal pleasures at your right hand.* - Psalm 16:11 (NIV)

MEDICAL MANAGEMENT

But God chose the foolish things of the world to shame the wise;

God chose the weak things of the world to shame the strong.

- 1 Corinthians 1:27 (NIV)

Doctors, Doctors and More Doctors

I quickly discovered that figuring out how to manage the delicate relationships with my child's doctors was one of the trickiest parts of the first year of a special needs diagnosis. Because I needed the doctors and specialists. I needed their knowledge and experience to diagnose, treat, prescribe, even do surgeries sometimes. But I struggled with needing their expertise while validating my instincts as mom. Then as I learned, one important aspect of advocacy is discerning whether or not the specialists' observations and assessment of my child's condition agrees with my momma instinct. The tension: They are the professionals. I am the mom. Both are significant roles.

If you're dealing with a special needs diagnosis, you'll meet all kinds of doctors. Some good listeners, humble and willing to work with you to come up with the best plan for your child. Some arrogant and aggressive and uncompromising.

We learned to trust our instincts when it came to doctors. In Year One, we had to change doctors when we suspected a doctor treating Nathan was missing something in his diagnosis. All of my mom red flags were going up, and my PA husband was also concerned. At our very first visit to a new doctor, the doctor said, "Yes, something's not right here." We left his office with the very diagnosis we suspected and a treatment plan.

Switching Doctors

If you want to switch doctors within the same office it can be a delicate matter. I suggest contacting the office manager, and explaining your dilemma. State that you would like to get in with another doctor in the practice. Explain the reason the doctor is not the best fit for your child and ask, "How would you suggest I handle this?" If you are unable to switch doctors, it may be time to

---

switch practices completely, if you live in a big enough city and have that luxury.

When you start talking to other parents about various specialists you begin to realize that everyone has an opinion of who's good and who's not good as practitioners. Sometimes you have consensus on opinions, sometimes not. I quickly realized from one particularly opinionated parent, that very few doctors met her criteria for her child. From another extremely laid back parent that it didn't matter much who her child saw because she was consistently okay taking their advice. I fall somewhere in the middle of those two extremes, weighing each doctor and medical issue separately.

A doctor who may be a good fit for one kid, might not be for yours. And vice versa. Try not to let other people's experiences taint your opinions too much. Instead, try to be unbiased and keep it to the medical facts of your kiddo. You are advocating for your kid, not someone else's.

Remember it's okay to ask lots of questions. It's okay to take up the doctor's time in order to get a full understanding of what's going on. Often you will feel rushed through an appointment but take advantage of the face-to-face time you have with them. Come prepared with your list of questions to ask. Show them your research on a particular diagnosis and get their opinion. Always ask them to further explain the treatment plan. Request they write down words you have never heard before. I am one of those crazy people who makes notes of what my child's doctor says during the appointment. I know that with everything going on in my brain I can't be trusted to remember what they said once I step over the threshold of the exam room. Plus, that way I can better re-explain it to my husband or research our conversation more later.

Make friends with the office staff. Especially the nurses as they can advocate for you when you need something from your specialist. At Christmastime, I brought a bunch of treats for staff. And I didn't go through a lot of work to do so. I went to Costco and bought a bunch of the festive goodies. That was all it took to have people remember me and my child.

Always say "Thank you." This seems obvious but I want my kiddo's doctors to know that I appreciate them. I may not always agree with them, but I respect their medical input and know how much they have helped my child in ways that I could not.

It's quite possible that the doctor's appointments will become fewer and further between as your child gets older. When you have a new diagnosis you often have a whole new set of specialists to manage that diagnosis, and it takes time to get established as a new patient. It also takes time to get organized with the many specialists.

In order to help with scheduling Nathan's appointments, I created a separate color in my Google calendar for him. This was a tip from a friend. That way I know things didn't conflict with one another. This also becomes helpful if you need to calculate mileage to and from doctor's visits for tax reasons.

I also made a list of all Nathan's specialists so that I didn't need to keep track of it all in my head. Casey's Circle has some helpful tools to keep you organized. I especially like the Medical Form Template. I use this as my one central document of information of doctors, diagnosis, medications and medical equipment. It helps me know which doctors are managing which issues and which ones are the most important.

Over time specialist appointments became fewer and fewer. We didn't get "discharged" from doctors because issues had not fully resolved, but we did get more and more of, "I'll see you in a year" follow-up requests, which is way better than, "I'd like to see him again next week." Getting past that first-year mark with doctor follow-ups made me feel like we had made significant strides. One caveat: one of Nathan's specialists got more and more frequent. So maybe it all balances out in the end.

Doctors are essential when you have a medically complex child. Many of them go into medicine because they want to help people and therefore they truly do mean well. Remember that, even when you don't feel like they "get it." The bottom line is it's not their child. It's yours.

Surgeries

Our son had two different surgeries and a handful of procedures requiring general anesthesia within his first year of life. Despite going through the routine several times, it does not get easier each time you do it.

You go through all of the pre-op work and are in the final minutes awaiting the hand-off to the operating room. It's the same feeling. You want to grab him back into your arms, say "Just kidding, I don't want to do this!" and run the other direction. But you don't. While your heart is saying, "Run the other way!" your mind is saying, "Just do it and don't look back. It's too awful."

Then you sit in the waiting room and you wait. And you wait and wait and wait. I bring a big bag of things to keep me occupied during that time. I try to look at it as quiet moments. Alone time for me to not have to care for any kids. I journal and pray and treat myself to a coffee. I try to make the most of it because once you are out of surgery, you are "on."

That was the biggest shock to me post-NICU. When your child is inpatient, whether on the floor, intermediate care, or the PICU you are a very critical component of the care team. You are expected to stay with your child at all times. It's not like at the NICU, where they shoo you away and promise to faithfully care for your baby. Here you advocate and fight to get what your child needs, which is usually the right pain meds.

Hospital Packing List

Packing for a hospital stay is most definitely not the same as packing for vacation. Think comfort, not cute. Here is a packing list to get you started based off some things you may experience in a hospital setting.

BATHROOM

Staying organized in the bathroom is key. You may get moved from one floor to another and you'll want to make moving rooms easy. Bring a small bin or tub to keep your toiletries in so they stay clean and easy to grab. The hospital is dry and you will be washing your hands a lot so don't forget things like eye drops and lotion to stay moisturized. You may also want to bring something aromatic to mask the smell of saved output. All output needs to get weighed or measured and it can stink. If you don't like cheap toilet paper and kleenex, bring your own. The hospital will provide towels.

- ❑ Toiletries
- ❑ Eye drops
- ❑ Lotion
- ❑ Bathrobe
- ❑ Lysol or essential oils diffuser
- ❑ Toilet paper
- ❑ Kleenex
- ❑ Feminine products
- ❑ Flushable wipes

BEDDING

It may be hard to sleep on a pull out couch or oversized chair, on top of being constantly interrupted throughout the night. Here are some things that might make it more cozy, especially if you are staying for a long time.

- ❑ Egg crate foam topper
- ❑ Sleeping bag or blanket (hospital blankets are thin and linty)
- ❑ Pillow

CLOTHES/SHOES

Again, think comfort. The hospital is cold and sterile, so dress accordingly.

- ❏ Slip on shoes or flip flops
- ❏ Comfortable clothes
- ❏ Sweater
- ❏ Socks

KIDS STUFF

This varies according to your child's age and needs, but here are some things to consider.

- ❏ Comfortable clothes
- ❏ Socks
- ❏ Blanket
- ❏ Special medical supplies, medications, formula, etc. that you think the hospital may not supply
- ❏ Favorite toys
- ❏ Entertainment: mobile, bubbles, shows/games on the tablet, mirror, books, music, etc.

ELECTRONICS

- ❏ Tablet or laptop (plus charger)
- ❏ Phone (plus charger)
- ❏ DVDs (many hospitals also have DVDs you can borrow)
- ❏ Mini speakers for music
- ❏ White noise machine
- ❏ Indoor extension cord

OTHER

- ❏ Tape, scissors, and paper, or a blanket. Something to block out the light coming through the window.
- ❏ Notepad or journal to take notes of who said what and questions you may have. You may also need to record concerning symptoms, names of visitors, etc.
- ❏ Snacks and drinks. Set up a little "station" of snacks. You can also place some things in the floor fridge as well.

You may also have unexpected hospital admissions. I keep a "Go Bag" and toiletry bag at the ready, just in case we are unexpectedly admitted. The Go Bag contains a set of all Nathan's medical supplies I need to make it through a twenty-four-hour period with my child. I can, and I have, grabbed it quickly in an emergency situation. The toiletry bag is of course for me. I know that I have the essentials of a toothbrush, hairbrush, and a place to put my contacts. I could sleep on a rock and be ready to go the next morning as long as I have fresh breath, combed hair and haven't worn my contacts all night long.

Therapy, Therapy and More Therapy

Therapy will likely become a way of life. It will become your sport. You'll go to therapy sessions. You'll do therapy homework intentionally at first. And eventually you'll find yourself doing something therapeutic without even realizing you're doing it. Therapy will change your perspective on development. Things you once took for granted, you'll begin to see as major accomplishments.

Since the whole world of therapy was new to me, I spent a lot of time researching the different models of therapy—educational model versus the medical model. Both have their usefulness. It's a matter of uncovering how to put together the best combination, or not, for your child. Also realizing that the therapy plan and professionals will likely change over time.

When your child is a baby through age three, the educational model is practiced through a state program called ECI, which stands for Early Childhood Intervention. This service came about through the Individuals with Disabilities Education Act (IDEA). Its overall purpose is to help children with delays and disabilities grow to be productive, independent individuals particularly as it relates to preparing them to enter the public school system. Once they reach age three they may be eligible to enter a preschool program through the public school.

The medical model of therapy addresses medical conditions to help a child realize his/her full potential. These are lifelong skills and do not solely pertain to education. Often the therapists will collaborate with your child's doctors to come up with a more comprehensive and long-term plan to maximize your child's development. The medical model tends to be more comprehensive in its scope.

Something I discovered early on is that my relationships with my son's therapists are very important to me. I wanted someone skilled and well-trained to work with him and educate me. I also wanted someone who I enjoyed working with, who listened to me and respected me, since it was to become such a significant portion of my schedule as well.

And the single biggest determinant of a good therapist in my opinion is whether or not the therapist believes in your child. If they talk more about the possibilities of your child, rather than the limitations, that's who I want to work with my son.

Therapy Questionnaire

There are several questions to ask when deciding on the therapist(s) and plan that are right for your child:

- ❏ Is the therapist able to communicate well with you? Do you have mutual understanding and respect? Do you have good chemistry?

- ❏ Do they have experience with your child's diagnosis? If your child's diagnosis is rare, do they have experience working with some of his/her specific symptoms?

- ❏ Can they describe what a therapy session will look like? Can they demonstrate how you will do some of the same therapies at home?

- ❏ Are they open to consulting with other therapists, doctors, and professionals?

- ❏ Will they push your child as far as you'd like and are comfortable with?

- ❏ Are they helping your child meet some of the goals established at the outset? Are the goals being re-evaluated periodically? Do you know what the goals

---

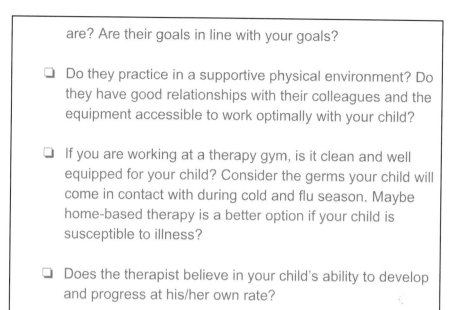

are? Are their goals in line with your goals?

❏ Do they practice in a supportive physical environment? Do they have good relationships with their colleagues and the equipment accessible to work optimally with your child?

❏ If you are working at a therapy gym, is it clean and well equipped for your child? Consider the germs your child will come in contact with during cold and flu season. Maybe home-based therapy is a better option if your child is susceptible to illness?

❏ Does the therapist believe in your child's ability to develop and progress at his/her own rate?

Know that it's okay to change therapists. I struggled with not wanting to burn bridges and lose touch of someone I liked, but at the same time, being proactive about getting my son what he needed within the realm of what was feasible for our family's schedule. Research the next therapist for your child using the questions above and remembering there's no perfect therapist, schedule, or location for all of this to happen. Use therapists you trust to network with and find the next therapist or therapy for your child.

If you are considering switching therapists, you should know that some insurance companies will only pay for one evaluation, or re-eval, for a certain term of time. For example our insurance requires a re-evaluation to qualify for services every six months, but will pay for no more than one during that six month term. So if I am wanting to switch OT services and my son just had a re-eval two months ago, the new agency may, or may not, be reimbursed by insurance for the new eval. They may try to pass that cost along to you. Make sense? I suggest marking on your calendar when the evals happen and then you can mentally prepare during the right times if you need to make a switch.

There are many alternative kinds of therapies—aqua therapy, music therapy, pet therapy, hippotherapy (horseback riding), corrective exercise therapy, and many others. With so many different things out there designed to help your child it's easy to get overwhelmed. How do you choose? Not everything is covered by insurance and not everything is as tried and true as the traditional PT, OT and ST therapies.

I recommend basing alternative therapy decisions on what your child responds to. My kiddo loves being in the water and he loves music. Both are calming to him. He likes dogs but tends to pull their hair really, really hard. Since my PT is willing to get in the neighborhood pool with him and teach me how to work his muscles we do a little aqua therapy. Eventually I would like to get him in some sort of music program but we just don't have the capacity for it right now. You know your child best. And if you wonder how they would respond to hippotherapy for example, call up a stable and see if you can bring your child by to get a sense of whether or not it would be a good fit.

Early on I liked going to therapy. It was my connection to the people who knew and cared for Nathan when he was inpatient. I liked that they knew his history and I didn't need to start all over telling them his story like I did with new doctors. We could pick up where we left off. I felt that somehow Nathan's therapists connected me to my support network through the most difficult time in my life. I needed to be grounded in that way.

Over time, however, therapy began to wear. me. out.

Once I began to accept that therapy was my special needs kid's version of an extracurricular activity, it wasn't as much a negative experience for me. I was taking my oldest to karate three times each week. Now I had another child who I took to therapy several times each week. It's all part of being a mom. Typical kiddo or special needs kiddo, you are going to spend a lot of time in the car.

A friend with an older child told me that eventually I could drop him off at therapy and either wait by myself in the waiting room or take off to get a quick coffee as a pick-me-up. A break for mom while your kid is working hard. At least I had this to look forward to...

That, and progress. I do see ways that my son has grown significantly because of therapy. That is rewarding. I haven't seen it daily or even weekly, but when I step back and look at where he was months ago, I can see that he is developing. It's on his own timeline with the help of therapists working hard to help him accomplish his goals.

SUPPORT/RESOURCES

Since they could not get him to Jesus because of the crowd, they made an opening in the roof above Jesus by digging through it and then lowered the mat the man was lying on. When Jesus saw their faith, he said to the paralyzed man, "Son, your sins are forgiven."

- Mark 2:4-5 (NIV)

Utilizing the Resources of a Children's Hospital

If you're lucky enough to be located in a city with a children's hospital, it could be of great help to you and your child. Your local children's hospital will likely offer a variety of resources for special needs and medically complex families. It's a matter of finding out how to access them. Since Nathan was essentially diagnosed at birth, we had the advantage of meeting some of these people and departments while he was still inpatient. Some of the most helpful and knowledgeable people were the case managers and social workers in the NICU, and then later, through the various specialists' offices. Most specialist groups, like neurology or outpatient hospital-based clinics, have social workers to help you navigate having a high-needs kiddo.

The best way I've found to make the most of the resources available at your children's hospital is utilizing the social workers. Social workers should be able to provide you with information on various state and federal programs for helping with medical costs and respite services. These programs are incredibly difficult to qualify for, but depending on your child's diagnosis and the level of severity of your case, you may be able to find aid to help your family in caring for your child. Social workers also put you in touch with local community support organizations. There are groups of parents who meet to share information and support one another.

Depending on how complex your child is medically, some parents opt for their child to become a patient of their a palliative care team. Palliative medicine is not just for end of life issues, but also for children who have a chronic and severe condition and who deal with ongoing pain. They can be the team of professionals who follow your child's medical care from a broader perspective. They can advocate for getting into various specialists sooner or pushing for certain tests. That has been extremely helpful for us with Nathan. At one point he was experiencing pain so bad that he needed to see a specialist quickly. The doctor's receptionist required us to wait an especially long time for an appointment, but our palliative care team was able to get him in to see the doctor much sooner.

Our local children's hospital's complex care clinic and palliative team hold regular educational sessions on various topics related to having a special needs child. Topics include: Guardianship, Therapy Dogs, Music as Therapy, Caregiver Stress, and Navigating the School System. We have learned so much through these educational meetings.

Other resources can be found through clinics. Complex care clinics and various other clinics use a team approach in caring for your child. Examples are Trach and Vent Clinic, Aerodigestive Clinic, Cystic Fibrosis Clinic, GI Clinic. These clinics can be especially helpful to you as you are able to meet with more than one specialist in a single visit, along with a dietician, therapist, and social worker. This condenses the amount of time that you spend at various different doctor's appointments. And, an all-around benefit, is that the doctors and other involved professionals can talk with each other, learn from each other about your child, and come up with a comprehensive approach in caring for your kiddo.

Your local children's hospital library may also be of service in finding resources and additional information—anything from finding information on your child's specific condition, to books for siblings, to researching the history of disability and civil rights. Having a librarian research something for you, you'll find information you wouldn't have thought to look for on your own.

All of these professionals at your children's hospital are eager to help you, so let them. You may come across some especially helpful nugget of information or invaluable resource.

Building a Support Structure of Special Needs Moms

As much as the help of professionals may be required, the support of fellow parents is essential. However, you do need to find the *right* people to talk to.

The best advice someone gave me early on was, "Choose your support very carefully." This advice came from a friend who is also an occupational therapist. She told me there were people who would provide me with hope and encouragement and all the good things I needed to make my way through these new and unknown challenges. And there were people that would make it miserable and rotten with their negativity and anger. She had seen this played out multiple times. I loved her advice because it was so true. It stuck with me as I navigated the community of special needs.

Early on I realized that the blogs from moms who had children with the same diagnosis as my son were not especially helpful for me to read. They were writing about daily life with a special needs child and all the challenges, like sleep deprivation, aggression and anxiety, with explicit detail. I wasn't ready to hear it. Honestly, I didn't need to hear it. I would go from having a decent day to reading a blog post and barely being able to pull it together and care for my children without crying. I wasn't ready to learn the day-to-day realities of other parents who had older kids with Nathan's syndrome. One day I was so blindsided by something another parent had written—something about a BM and a bathing suit--I had to call a friend. She came and took my oldest child out for the afternoon. I put the baby to bed and sat soaking in the bathtub for an hour. After that day, I vowed to not spend time on those blogs anymore.

Instead I found a very helpful website called Not Alone. A community of bloggers who are parents of children with special needs. The difference? They all have faith in a loving and sovereign God. They didn't sugar coat what they were going through, but they brought a perspective of truth and hope that I couldn't find in secular places.

Not much later I found a special needs moms' group through a local church. This was the type of group that I needed: a group of women with the same core beliefs and worldview who found solace in their similar circumstances of having a special needs child. Many of the women in the group were much further down the road than I was. I looked at them and found hope and inspiration. Sure they had been through alot with each of their different children, but they were still standing. That meant the world to me, just to know that life goes on. It's hard and challenging in ways different from other friends, but they still found enjoyment in their hobbies and in doing things together as a family.

Many different special needs diagnoses also have national associations. When Nathan was a few months old, we decided to become members of the national 5p-/Cri du Chat Society. This society represents my child's syndrome. I primarily wanted the membership directory so that I could find other families who lived nearby with the same diagnosis. I needed to talk to fellow moms. I needed to know if it was as bad as the textbooks and blogs told me. I needed to know what my life would look like, but I wanted to hear it from someone who was a fairly well-adjusted and emotionally healthy person. I didn't reach out to people right away, however.

An amazing thing happened. God began to put people in my path who knew of other parents with children who had the same diagnosis. First, my ECI case worker told me about a family nearby who had an older child. The caseworker knew the mom personally and assured me that she would be a helpful resource and willing to talk through some of the same challenges she faced especially in regards to Nathan's feeding issues.

Then, one day I was at Target and ran into an old friend. I briefed her on Nathan and all that was going on with him. She told me, "I feel like I've heard of that syndrome before." Eventually it clicked with her that her neighbor had a daughter with Cri du chat syndrome and that "she is very sweet." That was all I needed to hear to be okay with talking to her. As it turned out that family lives less than a mile away from us. A friendship blossomed over dinner and wine as we shared stories. Though they are very different kids with very different medical issues, our tears matched. They came from the same sorrows of having a baby who was different and who would always require so much extra from us as their mothers. My friendship with that mom has become a huge source of encouragement for me. She is a decade further down the road - a living example that life goes on and that you can still be you, even though your child is way different than you expected at the outset.

Building a support network of special needs parents is not much different from building a mom's group of neurotypical kids. There are people who are going to parent their special needs kids differently than you will, just as there are people who parent their typical developing children differently than you will. So just because your child has the same syndrome as mine doesn't mean that we'll instantly become best friends. Sometimes it turns into a beautiful and meaningful relationship, and sometimes not. It means that we are two different moms with two different kids and a little bit of overlap in our experiences. You aren't going to naturally click with everyone, simply because they are a special needs parent. However, you will intuitively know if you have a good connection. When you do, it's a beautiful thing.

It got so Nathan's NICU nurses, at first, then pediatrician and therapists would say to me, "I know a mom that I think you would connect well with, would you be willing to talk with her?" And of course I was. I began to build a network of individuals long before my son left the hospital and it has continued to grow long after he left.

Once your child's doctors know you are open to talking with other parents, they will often help make those connections for you and they can do so without violating HIPAA laws. Thank goodness, because those other parents provide a very unique way of understanding what parents of typical children cannot.

Finally I joined the closed Facebook page for Cri du chat syndrome. I resisted it for a long time. I resisted it for the very same reason I stopped reading other blogs. I didn't want to be depressed over something someone else's child was or wasn't doing when I didn't even know what my reality would be. The Facebook group has generally been positive for me. However, sometimes I find myself obsessing about something a parent said. That's when I have to check out for a while and go read truth and trust in my great, big God who is enough for all of the challenges—known and unknown—that we will face.

Now I am surprisingly finding myself in positions to offer support to other parents. By the time Nathan was six months old I had some experience that brand new mommas could benefit from. I'm still learning how to be the encouraging and supportive person to other people when there are still days I am kicking and fighting against this life of special needs. I don't always want to be the strong one. It's too much pressure. I'm learning that in my weakness, God is at work and enabling me to play the supporting role. I'm learning that authenticity and hope that rises above circumstances is often what I need when it comes to support. Maybe that's what others need as well.

Fighting Financial Stress

When our geneticist first sat us down to give us Nathan's diagnosis, the first thing that went through my head is, How am I going to be able to take care of him when I'm old? The second thing was, How in the world are we going to afford this? "This" being all of his medical care, special equipment, living expenses, and respite care givers.

Much in the same way I have been learning how to live day-by-day with the complexities of his diagnosis, I'm learning to live day-by-day financially. It is hard to trust that God is going to provide everything we need to help care for our son, but we are only a couple of years in and I have seen Him do it over and over again.

First, a group of friends decided to put together a fundraiser for the hospital expenses we had accrued from Nathan's two month NICU stay and all the follow-up therapies. It was incredibly humbling and surprising that people wanted to give to help us financially. I think people want to help and one of the easiest ways is for them to give is financially. If you are interested in fundraising for yourself or a loved one, I encourage you to check out Go Fund Me or You Caring.

Second, we decided to fight for disability services for Nathan even though that same geneticist who gave us the terrible, awful, no good news also told us we wouldn't qualify for financial services. God opened doors despite the odds that we would not receive help. Public funding is another clear example of how He provides in tangible ways.

I have come to fully believe that God gave me Nathan with all of his complex medical mysteries and challenges. Therefore, why would He not graciously provide all that we need in order to be able to care for him? It is a decision and an opportunity to trust God.

Navigating Government Programs

Each state offers different disability services. I can't speak to every state. The <u>Kids' Waivers</u> website should provide you information specific for your state. The best advice I can offer is ask questions. Lots of questions. And be persistent. Keep applying, keep calling, and keep asking and waiting and expecting answers.

Social workers will be the most informative people in navigating the confusing world of public aid. Sometimes they know more than the government representatives because they work closely with the people requiring services. Use your social worker at the hospital, specialists, or work through your local early intervention program.

You should know within a few months whether or not your child is a good candidate. And if they aren't at that time, ask about waiting lists, lotteries, and waiver programs for services. It may be a fight worth fighting.

Finding Respite Caregivers

In the beginning people will come out of the woodwork to offer help and support. They rush to your side in support of your family. They come bearing gifts, and bringing meals, they willingly listen to your tears, hold your heart gently as it's breaking, and babysit your kids while you go out to take a break. Over time, however, life goes on. Some of them develop compassion fatigue and who can blame them? They have their own families, their own problems.

Your true friends reveal themselves however. Those who are in it for the long haul. They become part of a sacred family and web of support. They hold you up in prayer when you can't utter a word to God. They say things that help you get through an especially hard day. They remain kind, even when you can't be the same reciprocal friend as you were in the past. And they don't judge you, they simply accept you as you are. This friendship is a great gift.

You are going to continue to need help. It doesn't matter if your child is low functioning and dependent on medical interventions, or high functioning with very few medical issues. You are going to need not just a physical break, but an emotional break from your kiddo. You don't have to do everything. You will be a better parent because you received help.

We received various forms of respite help from people during Nathan's first couple of years. In many ways it's easy to get help when your child is a baby. Who doesn't want to hold a sweet sleeping baby? That's what many of our friends did for us. They would let me run out for a quick errand, take an especially long shower, or give my husband and me a few hours for a date night.

Through Nathan's disability services we qualified for nursing help. At first I wasn't so sure I was comfortable having a stranger in my home caring for my son. However, I worked with the nursing agency to find someone we had good chemistry with. I started out by having her come when my oldest was in preschool. During that time I could be home in case anything would happen. It made me feel better to be there. As we built trust I was able to venture out and leave her with the care of my son.

Later on we were able to hire respite workers for my son. This allowed me to have friends and people who I knew and trusted care for my son. I simply trained them to feed him and give him his medications.

You may think that you can do it all on your own without the help of another caregiver. And maybe you can. That's what I thought. I quickly learned that I needed help in order to flourish as a person apart from my son. Budgeting for regular respite help has been one of the biggest investments we've made in our family.

EMOTIONAL MANAGEMENT

There is an appointed time for everything.

And there is a time for every event under heaven—

A time to weep and a time to laugh;

A time to mourn and a time to dance.

- Ecclesiastes 3:1,4 (NASB)

Waves of Grief

The grief cycle is different for everyone. Some say that you start at denial and end at acceptance. I don't know that it looks so smooth for special needs parents, or anyone for that matter. Everyone grieves differently. It's messy and miserable and seemingly unending. I don't know that grief ever fully goes away when you are a special needs parent. As Pearl Buck[2] said in *The Child Who Never Grew*, you "learn how to bear it."

She went on to say,

> For there are basically two kinds of sorrows: those which can be assuaged and those which cannot be. The death of parents is sad, for they cannot be replaced, but it is not the inescapable sorrow. It is natural sorrow. It is natural sorrow, that which one must expect in the normal course of life. The crippling of one's body, irremediably, is an inescapable sorrow. It has to be lived with; and more than that, it has to be used for some other sort of life than that planned in health. The sorrows which can be assuaged are those which life can cover and heal. Those which cannot be assuaged are those which change life itself and in a way themselves make life. Sorrows that can die can be assuaged, but living sorrow is never assuaged. 'It is a stone thrown into the stream,' as Browning put it, 'and the water must divide itself and accommodate itself, for it cannot remove the stone.'

I didn't find these words particularly comforting, but they were honest and they resonated deep in my heart. They legitimized my experience of grief which was so different from anything I had experienced before. Buck's words gave me a vague direction of going forward, of living in light of who my son is and who he will become.

I think you can come to acceptance of some particular thing about your child. Then, a transition or new development or aspect of your child's disability throws you into a tailspin. You end up somewhere in the cycle all

73

over again. So, even though grief is unsuspecting, I do know there are healthy ways to cope and that you will have to do so over and over again.

Stay in grief too long and you become an island. It's lonely, and easy to grow a bitter root. You can quickly dip into depression and self-pity.

Deny grief and it surfaces like a volcano. Angry outbursts at people not responsible for your pain happen unexpectedly.

To deal with grief in a healthy way is hard work. Because grief surfaces at unusual times and places. As much as you can, you have to be prepared and well-equipped to face it when it comes.

Sometimes grief will hit me when I'm in public, watching another child the same age as mine walk, and speak, and interact with his mother in a way mine isn't. I feel the sorrow to the extent that I can in that moment, which is usually only a little bit, and then let myself have a good cry when I'm alone.

Sometimes it hits me in those rare moments when I am all by myself and it's quiet. I've woken to reality many times in the early morning or from an afternoon nap with a well of sadness, deep in the pit of my stomach. I try to stay in the feeling for a moment and pray my way through it. If I acknowledge the feeling, it lingers far less than if I try to suppress it.

Sometimes when I am in the presence of a trusted friend, my grief comes to the surface. When it happens in the presence of a person who can witness it, affirm it, and speak truth into it, I can go forward more confidently. And the blessing of this kind of grief processing is that I have a person bearing the pain along with me.

You'll learn over time how to grieve well. You'll learn the balance between acknowledging the sadness and loss and also joyfully functioning as a parent to your kids, a wife or a husband to your spouse, and a person in society. If you are open to it, you'll learn more of God's character going through hard things. In the midst of it, you will find things that bring you peace.

Prayer brings me peace. Worship music brings me peace, especially while exercising. Writing brings me peace. These things enable me to return to the real, hard work of the rest of the world. The world won't understand everything you are going through, but God does. Psychologists swear by the stages of grief. I stand by the grace of God as the waves of grief overcome me and then subside. I expect it to be a lifetime of riding those waves, knowing I am never alone. Feeling His presence as I invite Him into the process.

> *We are hard pressed on every side, but not crushed; perplexed, but not in despair; persecuted, but not abandoned; struck down, but not destroyed. We always carry around in our body the death of Jesus, so that the life of Jesus may also be revealed in our body. For we who are alive are always being given over to death for Jesus' sake, so that his life may also be revealed in our mortal body. So then, death is at work in us, but life is at work in you.* - 2 Cor 4:8-12 (NIV)

Acceptance and Longing for Something More

The day we received Nathan's diagnosis was hands-down the worst day of my life. No little girl dreams of growing up and having a child who will be in a wheelchair, unable to walk, cognitively impaired and unable to get a job, made fun of. This was not my plan for the perfect family and life that I envisioned.

I tried to muster up enough "raw courage" to deal with Nathan's diagnosis. God quickly showed me that I could not do it on my strength alone. During Nathan's stay in the NICU, he "coded" three times. The first time I wasn't there. My husband was. I remember the phone call I received from him late one night, "He's not good, Kathy. He completely stopped breathing for a couple of minutes. The whole respiratory team came rushing to his bedside. They ran code on him and it took about thirty minutes for him to regain color. He's not good." he repeated. My response was to muster up something vaguely encouraging to say to my husband. Then roll over and go back to sleep. My body was being pushed to the max as were my emotions and my faith. My ability to process Nathan's condition was overwhelming. I was shutting down.

> *But he said to me, 'My grace is sufficient for you, for my power is made perfect in weakness." Therefore I will boast all the more gladly about my weaknesses, so that Christ's power may rest on me. That is why, for Christ's sake, I delight in weaknesses, in insults, in hardships, in persecutions, in difficulties. For when I am weak, then I am strong. - 2 Cor 12: 9-11 (NIV)*

During another one of Nathan's episodes of respiratory distress I was pushed aside in the midst of all the nurses, respiratory therapists, and doctors swarming his bed. As they were working on him I felt the presence of God overwhelm me. It was a very different kind of overwhelmed. I wasn't overwhelmed by my circumstances as much as I was by the power and presence of God. It was very clear He was asking me, "Can you give Me control? Control over the life of your son? Over your life and what it

77

will look like with a special needs kid?"

I knew that I needed to hand over my perfect plan for my baby to God. I couldn't control whether or not he would live past the first year of his life. Or, who would take care of him if he were to outlive me. I simply needed to trust in God's greater plan and purposes.

The Mystery of My Son

When Nathan entered my life I couldn't help but think of him as a mystery. I wanted to put all the pieces together and uncover the bigger picture of not just his body, but his life and his purpose. I wanted to answer the question, why? I didn't understand why his body was born broken, why God had given him to me, and why we were continually uncovering medical mysteries?

John Piper[6] writes in *Suffering and the Sovereignty of God*:

> Suffering itself is a mystery. This is why the Bible tells us to see now by faith. Though suffering is a mystery to us, it is not a mystery to God. Mysteries may be painful, but they should not perplex us. To God, there is no mystery. He is satisfied because he sees the whole ledger. We will also be satisfied when we see things from God's perspective. Till then, we must learn to be satisfied with God's satisfaction. If we do, we will have peace.

There are simply too many unknowns. I don't get to make up my own plan for my son's life. God does. Everything started to change as I began to acknowledge His Sovereignty—that He is good, that He has a plan, and that He knew this all along.

While Nathan was still in the NICU I began to pray through the verse, "Call to me and I will answer you and tell you great and unsearchable things you do not know." (Jeremiah 33:3 NIV) I am still not privy to all the mysteries of God, but by praying that verse I have begun to see more clearly how He is working through the things I don't understand to teach me more about Himself.

Through Nathan entering my life, my view of God has changed. I have been more willing to trust in His goodness and his purposes over my own. I may not understand what He is doing, but I know I can't go against him with my own measly attempts to control my circumstances. I know that there is power in submitting to Him, even when it's hard, and staying close to Him, depending on Him for everything I need.

The Why Question

So what do we do with the "Why?" question anyway?

Grief commonly causes you to ask the question, Why? Why did this happen? Why me? Why my son? This question will lead you right back into the grief cycle all over again. As I said before I do believe that that grief will return again (though perhaps not as hard as it does initially). If you keep asking the why question however, you may keep ending up back at the same place unnecessarily. It's an honest question but it's likely not going to give you an answer that's all that satisfying this side of eternity.

In a sermon the summer Nathan was born our pastor, Matt Cassidy, Phd.[4], encouraged us to courageously ask the question "How long?" This question will begin to form a new perspective on life, and death, and eternity.

> *But as it is, they desire a better country, that is, a heavenly one. Therefore God is not ashamed to be called their God; for He has prepared a city for them.* - Hebrews 11:16 (NASB)

For those of us who believe in Jesus, that He made a way for us to enter into a better "country" with Him in heaven, we have a hope of things to come. The focus becomes less on "Why?" and more on "How Long?" When O Lord, will my son be healed? When will I not feel pain over his pain? When will he be fully accepted for who he is? When will there be no more tears for what this disability has taken from us?

He will wipe every tear from their eyes; and there will no longer
be any death: there will no longer be any mourning, or crying, or
pain; the first things have passed away. - Revelation 21:4 (NASB)

When you ask the question of "How long?" you turn your eyes to Jesus, instead of asking "Why?" which keeps the focus on you.

Those of us who have been given a child with special needs have been given access to another level of living entirely. Before Nathan was born I longed to arrange my life in such a way that I could be as comfortable as possible and safe and secure here on earth. I did so without even fully realizing it.

After Nathan I realized there was no real comfort in this world. The inescapable sorrow of having a child with disabilities would soon affect how I live my life in a way that was completely uncomfortable. My hope, however, was and is, being transformed from an earthly hope of striving for perfection here, to a hope found in heaven. My child will be made whole in heaven one day. We all will be whole. How I long for that day.

> "No other religion, no other philosophy promises new bodies, hearts, and minds. Only in the Gospel of Christ do hurting people find such incredible hope." - Joni Eareckson Tada[7]

We are spiritual beings in physical bodies. I know that for certain when I look at Nathan. The way he intensely looks into my eyes, it's as if his spirit sees straight into mine. His look forces me to examine myself and admit own limitations, my inability to love well. I see him differently too. When I pray out loud, he becomes very still and listens with his whole being. I wonder if deep in his spirit he understands things I may not.

I love this passaged excerpted from *Heaven* by Randy Alcorn[1]:

Whenever I spend time with severely handicapped people—physically, mentally, or both—I'm keenly aware of how wonderful it will be to have resurrected bodies. My friend David O'Brien is a brilliant man trapped in a body that groans for redemption. His cerebral palsy will be gone the moment he leaves this world for the intermediate Heaven, but the biggest treat will be at his resurrection, when he will have a new body, forever free of disease. I picture David never having to repeat himself because others don't understand him. I see him running through fields on the New Earth. I look forward to running beside David...and probably behind him.

I often think of how paraplegics, quadriplegics, and people who have known constant pain will walk, run, jump, and laugh in the New Earth. Believers who are blind now will gawk at the New Earth's wonders. What a special pleasure for them.

We can become so distracted by the things of this world. Having a child with special needs contains a rare gift however. The experience of parenting a child with special needs has the potential to turn your eyes upward. If you do look for true Hope, found in accepting the person of Jesus Christ as payment for your sin, you will be completely transformed by His grace both now, and for all of eternity.

For all have sinned and fall short of the glory of God, and all are justified freely by his grace through the redemption that came by Christ Jesus.
Romans 3:23-24 (NIV)

OWNING IT

Then Jesus said to his host, "When you give a luncheon or dinner, do not invite your friends, your brothers or sisters, your relatives, or your rich neighbors; if you do, they may invite you back and so you will be repaid. But when you give a banquet, invite the poor, the crippled, the lame, the blind, and you will be blessed. Although they cannot repay you, you will be repaid at the resurrection of the righteous."

- Luke 14:12-14 (NIV)

Looking Forward - Anticipating Hard Things

We are still uncovering mysteries of Nathan and how God made his fragile little body. There are all sorts of medical abnormalities about Nathan that puzzle even the experts. His heart is not in the correct position in his chest. He has kidney reflux, which means urine is going back up into his kidneys and causing damage, and his right kidney is very small and has stopped growing completely. He has a strange spot on the back of his head that looks like his brain is growing out through the back of his skull on an MRI. He needed surgery for a tethered spinal cord, surgery for his eyes which were turning outward, and surgery to correct his gastroesophageal reflux.

Of all his medical complications, eating is the hardest one for me as his mother. He simply cannot manage the coordination needed to swallow, and therefore aspirates when he tries to eat by mouth. We reluctantly decided to put in a feeding tube at five weeks old so he receives nutrition directly to his stomach. No one can give me an answer as to whether or not he will ever eat by mouth.

I've also spent a lot of time—a LOT of time—worrying about the emotional and behavioral things associated with my son's diagnosis. Common symptoms of having a son with disabilities: not able to sleep through the night, aggressive with others, harmful to himself, hyperactive.

I deeply fear the judgment of others. Having people pity me because of my son's disability. Or, people thinking it was my fault that his behavior was so inappropriate and unmanageable. I think his behavior is my biggest fear. Fear that I'll have no control over him and we'll be locked away together because society isn't ready for him.

I started to realize that in all these fears the thing I most needed to come to terms with was my fear of myself. Fear of not being able to mother my son. So many times I would research group homes and residential schools. I would devise back-up plans in my head. I was simply drowning in my inability to manage my son and his diagnosis.

It finally dawned on me. This fear is a huge form of pride that I think it's up to me to have all of it figured out. I'm not God. I don't know the future or how things will play out. Only He does. And He's offering Himself to me as the One and only source of everything I need. From peace deep in my spirit to financial resources. From restorative sleep to behavior management tools.

As I began to pray about my fears, God challenged me to stop problem solving and let Him provide. *I will provide* became the most common answer to my prayers. I still don't have all the answers I'd like, but I'm learning to live in today, not the future. Living and depending on a loving God providing everything that I need *day-by-day*.

> *Therefore we do not lose heart. Though outwardly we are wasting away, yet inwardly we are being renewed day by day. For our light and momentary troubles are achieving for us an eternal glory that far outweighs them all. So we fix our eyes not on what is seen, but on what is unseen, since what is seen is temporary, but what is unseen is eternal.* - 2 Cor 4:16-18 (NIV)

I began to see that God was writing a beautiful story into my life and my family. I was so focused on the things seen here in this world. I was looking for perfection and comfort and happiness here on earth where things rot and decay and are temporary. God is focused on the things which are unseen. And all of the hard things in this life—including my son's very broken body—He is using for a great purpose. God's grander plan is preparing me for eternity with Him one day when everything will be redeemed and resurrected and made perfect.

> "When you're on the New Earth, for the first time you'll be the person God created you to be."
> -Randy Alcorn

I still struggle with so many questions about how I will ever care for my child—physically, financially, emotionally. But I'm accepting more and more that I don't have to work hard to come up with a plan. And ultimately, I'm accepting that it doesn't have to look perfect. I just need to live day-by-day with God.

You can't know the future of your life on earth. You can know the future of your life eternally. By trusting in Jesus to stand absolutely perfectly before God on your behalf so that you will be prepared to enter a far better, more perfect place.

1. What are your biggest fears?

2. Have you been able to find hope in the person of Jesus? If so, how?

Looking Back - Remembering the Good Things and Milestones

I wish I was a glass-half-full sort of a person. Not only do I see the glass half-empty, but I can visualize it falling from the table onto the floor and shattering into a million pieces. Then as I'm picking up the mess stepping on shards that are cutting my feet to pieces. Yeah, I can make it bad in my mind. Real bad.

That's why remembering and recording the good days is essential.

After Nathan was born, everything seemed darker in my world. I had a hard time seeing any hope or beauty as a result of his diagnosis. I lived and breathed the pain from his condition almost constantly.

I do remember one Saturday evening we went out to dinner as a family to a local family restaurant that we love. It had only been a matter of weeks since we brought Nathan home from the hospital. He slept in my arms practically through the entire meal. He was cuddly and sweet and no one knew there was anything wrong with him. For once, we were a normal family and I could completely let go of all of my burdens in order to fully enjoy that meal. I went to bed that night so full of gratitude, so satisfied. Nothing seemed wrong in my world that night. I remember being so, so grateful for that moment. Things did get harder after that, but at least I had that memory to go back to and meditate on and hold closely in my heart.

Remembering the Good Things and Milestones

I began to list the good things that came out of the first year of Nathan's life and I highly recommend this exercise. It was so helpful for me to see the positives after an incredibly difficult year.

Here's a peek at some our good memories born from a hard year.

- We met some of the most caring, compassionate, patient, and understanding people on the planet. I never knew they existed, specifically the staff we met while in the NICU. I still keep in touch with some of the nurses, they became a sort of extended family to us.

- Homecoming Day. The day Nathan came home from the NICU felt almost as significant as his birthday. We were no longer living in Room 6 of the NICU. My baby was finally ready for the nursery I had prepared for him.

- Help from friends and family with things like: meals, holding Nathan in the NICU, bringing groceries, hosting playdates for our firstborn, mowing our lawn. You name the need, they met it.

- First Holidays. Christmas, Easter, and all the pictures of my boys *together*.

- First Birthday. We celebrated Nathan's first birthday by running a 5K to raise money for sMiles4Sammy and for all other families who will follow along behind us.

- Writing and speaking. I was able to share my story, which helped not only me process what I was going through, but others as well. Sharing our story helped my pain make more sense. I knew it was not in vain that we suffered but for God's greater glory.

- Nathan's first smile. I'll never forget it. And the other developmental things that for him were a really big deal like the first roll, first reach, first intentional sound.

The thing with many special needs children is that when they do develop, they don't always master it and never look back. It's a path of development that's filled with many twists and turns and false starts. Everything is dependent on how they are feeling and whether or not they're able to manage everything in their environment. Their little bodies vary so much from day-to-day.

I'm beginning to see when I put in 110% of the work with Nathan, I get 110% back. Maybe not right away, but in time. It comes in the quiet, still moments of the morning when I look deep into his eyes. I see the reflection of his soul. I know he is deep in there. I know I am not supposed to give up or give in or cop out. I need to keep going. I know that as much as I do all this for him, he is blessing me.

1. What are some of the good things/blessings that have come out of your child's life?

2. What do you what to remember about this first year?

Living in Today

What might you be missing in this moment because you are trying to live in the future?

It's a discipline for me to live in the moment. After reading Ann Voskamp's[9] book, *One Thousand Gifts*, I learned that gratitude enabled me to be more present. I began to look for things to be thankful for throughout my day. Sometimes they were big and obvious. *Nathan rolled over. We got a full night's sleep.* Sometimes they were so subtle I may have missed them. *The morning sunlight streaming through my family room next to my baby on his playmat. Mac willingly running to get a diaper for me.*

I still try to make a goal of at least three things I'm thankful for each day. I keep a pretty little notebook near my computer and jot down some nuggets of gratitude each morning. It's one of my favorite parts of the day. I look forward to seeing God's goodness in my life. It's helpful for me to focus on what He's doing right now. Today.

So live in today. Live in today knowing if and when you face overwhelming challenges, you will overcome. You will be creative, resourceful, resilient. You will see God provide.

1. What are you thankful for today?

2. List three things you are thankful for each and every day.

3. Pray for the future, but pray especially for today.

Therefore do not worry about tomorrow, for tomorrow will worry about itself. Each day has enough trouble of its own. - Matthew 6:34 (NIV)

RECONCILING IT

And we know that God causes all things to work together for good to those who love God, to those who are called according to His purpose.

- Romans 8:28 (NASB)

Ways to Give Back

Even though I had no time, energy, or resources to give back in that first year, it was helpful for me to brainstorm ways that I could eventually. As much as I hated the NICU for all of the medical procedures and lack of bonding for my baby, I loved it for the nurses who cared for and loved on my son when I couldn't. One of the most significant things to me was how they loved him. So I thought, "Hey, I could do that. I could go in and hold babies. I could sew blankets for NICU babies. I could bring gifts back to the NICU during the holidays, become a peer mentor to someone going through a similar diagnosis, fundraise, blog." There are so many more.

Once you have gone through the rough waters of receiving a special needs diagnosis, you are much more able to empathize with others who are going through difficult circumstances of their own.

> *Praise be to the God and Father of our Lord Jesus Christ, the Father of compassion and the God of all comfort, who comforts us in all our troubles, so that we can comfort those in any trouble with the comfort we ourselves receive from God. For just as we share abundantly in the sufferings of Christ, so also our comfort abounds through Christ. - 2 Cor 1: 3-5 (NIV)*

Sometimes it's helpful to dream of ways you can give back. Or simply just do them. Comforting others is an opportunity to rise above your circumstances and provide hope to another person in need. This is your one life. Life it fully wherever you're at. For me, it's writing. Sometimes needs arise where I can cook a meal for someone or hand deliver a coffee and a listening ear. Who knows, maybe one day I'll even get to go back and hold those babies.

1. What could you do? What do you want to do?

2. What unique experience or perspective do you have to offer to someone else in need?

Imagining Life Beyond the First Year

I stand here more than a year out from my son's special need diagnosis. In some ways it's completely surreal that this is my life. This is the thing that happens to other people, not me. But it did. It happened to me. And now I am forced into that reality daily. It's still jolting. I still struggle to accept this lot.

BUT.

The grief I experienced initially isn't as powerful as it was then. It still comes in waves. It's unexpected and sweeps me off my feet at times. But I'm able to get back up more quickly. I have tools and people in place to help me get through those hard moments.

The single biggest help has come from my faith in God. In knowing that this world is not all there is. There is hope of a perfect, whole life in heaven because of my belief in Jesus. I look to Him. He lived a perfect life. He suffered and died on the cross. By believing in His suffering and sacrifice of Himself made a way for me. He graciously offers His perfection and righteousness to me through faith so that I can be with Him eternally.

You've heard the phrase "life goes on." And it does. I think we often say that to mean everyone else's life goes on while you are stuck in this purgatory that you can't get out of. I'm here to tell you that yours goes on as well. You will find joy again. And in some ways the depth of pain you experience allows you to experience greater joy as well. You take joy in the little things. The everyday miracles.

> "Your joy is your sorrow unmasked...the deeper the sorrow carves into your being, the more joy you can contain." -Kahlil Gibran[5]

One of the greatest expressions of joy I've found is in my typical son who when he runs across a room I think, "Wow, his legs work." Or, when he won't stop talking from the backseat of the car I am grateful that he knows how to verbalize things so incredibly well. The fact that he's potty trained is something I took for granted before.

When I work out really hard, I can't help but praise God for how my body works. I can do things like run, cycle, lift weights, and groceries, and my kids. I can eat food by mouth. These are things my son may never accomplish. These are the everyday miracles that we are meant to rejoice in just as much as the amazing stories.

Not Losing You

Am I still the same person? In some ways yes. I still love my coffee with cream, burying my nose in a good book, sanguine music, a neatly organized closet, bargain hunting for clothes, a good hard work-out, a spring hike with my family, and watching the sun set on the beach with my husband. I still need to make time for those things I enjoy.

In some ways no, I am not the same person. I know how to work feeding pumps, mix medicines, give enemas, and insert a catheter into my son so he can pee. And I know a whole lot more about therapy and sensory issues. My role is certainly different than it was one year ago. I am not just mom, but carer. I am a nurse-mom.

It's easy to let your children become your identity if you let them.

I feel different but I also feel the same.

Eventually I will have to move out of the old me/new me mode of thinking. I think it's good to reflect on from time to time, but eventually I just need to accept me and all that God's brought into my life.

A dear friend sent me a book called, *Just Being Audrey*, not long after Nathan was born. She wrote me a note that said, "This book reminded me of you. It's for you. Read it to yourself sometime to remember to give yourself grace and love and to practice at times, 'Just Being Kathy.'"

She wanted me to still be me in spite of Nathan completely altering my life. She bought it because I loved everything Audrey Hepburn before Nathan was born and I love everything Audrey after Nathan. I love her big brown eyes, her classic fashion and the way she carries herself with elegance and grace.

In her classic movie, *Breakfast at Tiffany'* Hepburn plays the role of a frightened young woman living a completely meaningless life. She talks about having not just the blues, but the mean reds. This year has brought on a lot of the mean reds.

However, I'm not the same scared, shallow girl I started out as last year. My life actually has taken on way more meaning that I ever expected. I am passionate about people knowing my son, and other people with disabilities. I'm passionate about others knowing these special individuals so they don't miss what God is trying to teach us through them. Mostly I'm compelled by telling the truth so that God will be glorified.

> *Jesus answered, "It was neither that this man sinned, nor his parents; but it was so that the works of God might be displayed in him."* - John 9: 3 (NASB)

The answer that Jesus gives has nothing to do with the cause—with the whys, with what we do or don't do—the answer has everything to do with God's greater purposes.

> *It was so that the works of God might be displayed in him.* - John 9: 3 (NASB)

Can you believe that? Something that is so terribly devastating like a little boy who is very disabled, even that, can be made into something beautiful. God is displaying His works through Nathan. He may not heal him on earth, and I believe that He could, but he will be fully healed, fully made perfect, in heaven. How I long for that day.

CONCLUSION

"So the last will be first, and the first will be last."

- Matthew 20:16 (NIV)

The first year of a special needs diagnosis is hard. Incredibly hard. In some ways it gets easier once you get past the one year mark, some ways it gets harder. All in all, it is just different. Life is forever changed. You have to determine how you will go forward. Or not.

So, is it over yet? No. Probably not. It may be just the beginning. But keep asking the question "How long, O Lord?" as you look to Him to guide you through the next chapter. He will give you the grace to respond to circumstances you have no control over. And through it you will learn amazing things about yourself, your child, and other people.

It may not be the life that you dreamed of when you were a little girl, but it's your life. Despite the fact that it doesn't look picture perfect, and your best dreams may be broken, it still can be dramatically beautiful.

You have been given a high calling friend.

In the beginning days of Nathan's NICU stay I found this:

> *Trust in the Lord and do what is right!*
> *Settle in the land and maintain your integrity!*
> *Then you will take delight in the Lord and he will answer your prayers.*
> *Commit your future to the Lord!*
> *Trust in him, and he will act on your behalf.*
> *He will vindicate you in broad daylight, and publicly defend your*

just cause.
Wait patiently for the Lord!
Wait confidently for him! - Psalm 37: 3-7 (NET)

What am I to do? Trust God and settle into the place of my circumstances. Whatever He has set before me, commit my future to God and wait patiently and confidently for Him to act.

What does God promise to do? Answer my prayers. Act on my behalf. Vindicate me and defend me. He is coming for me and my son. One day we will all be made whole.

> "My hope is not in the absence of suffering and comfort returned. My hope is in the presence of the One who promises never to leave or forsake, the One who declares nothing can separate you from my love. Nothing." - Kara Tippets[8]

Photo Credit: Markum Photography

APPENDIX

Notes

[1] Alcorn, Randy. *Heaven*. (Wheaton, Ill.: Tyndale, 2004).

[2] Buck, Pearl, *The Child Who Never Grew*. (New York, NY: The John Day Company; First Edition, 1950).

[3] Cardillo, Margaret, *Just Being Audrey*. (New York, NY: Balzer + Bray, an imprint of HarperCollins Publishers, 2011).

[4] Cassidy, Matthew, PhD, "Lament," from the sermon series *Everyday Worship*, July 2013, http://grace360.org/th_gallery/everyday-worship/

[5] Gibran, Kahlil. *The Prophet*. (New York, NY: Alfred A. Knopf, 1923).

[6] Piper, John and Tony Reinke, *Disability and the Sovereign Goodness of God*. (Minneapolis, MN: Desiring God, 2012, http://www.desiringgod.org/books/disability-and-the-sovereign-goodness-of-god).

[7] Tada, Joni Eareckson, *Joni: An Unforgettable Story*. (Grand Rapids, MI: Zondervan, 2010).

[8] Tippets, Kara, *The Hardest Peace: Expecting Grace in the Midst of Life's Hard*. (Colorado Springs, CO: David C. Cook, 2014).

[9] Voskamp, Ann, *One Thousand Gifts*. (Grand Rapids, MI: Zondervan, 2011).

Additional Resources

For more recommended books on disability, visit <u>My Favorite Books</u> on, <u>All Things Beautiful</u>.

<u>Websites</u>

All Things Beautiful - http://kathymcclelland.com/

Caseys Circle - http://caseyscircle.org/

Complex Child - http://complexchild.org/

Ellen Stumbo - http://www.ellenstumbo.com/

Feeding Tube Awareness Foundation - http://www.feedingtubeawareness.org/

Grace Without Margins Disability Education and Training - http://gracewithoutmargins.com/

Hand to Hold - http://handtohold.org/

Joni and Friends - http://www.joniandfriends.org/

Key Ministry - http://www.keyministry.org/

Kids' Waivers - http://kidswaivers.org/

Live Better with Disability - http://www.livebetterwithdisability.com/

March of Dimes - http://www.marchofdimes.org/

Mommies of Miracles - http://mommiesofmiracles.com/

Navigate Life Texas - https://www.navigatelifetexas.org

Not Alone - http://specialneedsparenting.net/

PreemieBabies101 - http://www.preemiebabies101.com/

sMiles4Sammy - http://www.smiles4sammy.org/

The Mighty - https://themighty.com/

Author Bio

 **Kathy McClelland** is momma to two precious boys. Her second son was born with a rare (1 in 50,000 births) chromosomal disorder. She blogs at <u>KathyMcclelland.com</u> about finding beauty and hope in the midst of broken dreams. She is also a regular contributor to <u>PreemieBabies101.com</u> and has published on <u>TheMighty.com</u>, <u>EllenStumbo.com</u> and <u>Sparkhouse.org</u>. Her free time activities are not as often as she would like, but when she can she likes to cycle away stress, wander Target aimlessly, and camp out at coffee shops. Slowly she is learning that God makes ***all things beautiful*** in His time, even when life doesn't turn out picture perfect as she hoped.

Help Spread the Word

If you found this book helpful, and if you think someone else may benefit from hearing the stories of God making broken things beautiful, please share.

More stories of finding hope and beauty in the midst of broken dreams can be found at:
kathymcclelland.com

86394478R00061

Made in the USA
Lexington, KY
11 April 2018